Why You Are Poor

A Brutally Honest Look at the Habits,
Beliefs, and Systems That Keep You Broke

All Rights Reserved

Why You Are Poor: A Brutally Honest Look at the Habits, Beliefs, and Systems That Keep You Broke

© 2025 Zen Hunter

Published by Dofil Press

No part of this publication may be reproduced, distributed, stored in a retrieval system, or transmitted in any form or by any means, including electronic, mechanical, photocopying, recording, or otherwise, without the prior written permission of the author and publisher, except as permitted by law.

This book is provided for informational and educational purposes only. Although the author and publisher have made every effort to ensure the accuracy and completeness of information contained in this publication, they assume no responsibility for errors, inaccuracies, omissions, or any inconsistency herein. Readers are responsible for applying their own judgment and discretion.

All trademarks mentioned herein are the property of their respective owners.

For permissions, inquiries, or further information, please contact:

Dofil Press
Dofil.co.uk

First Edition, 2025

"Your daily habits decide if you stay poor, middle class, or become wealthy."

Contents

Introduction 7

Chapter 1 : The Poverty Programming   11

Chapter 2 : Comfort Is Killing You   15

Chapter 3 : Excuses That Keep You Broke   19

Chapter 4 : Your Environment Is Poison   23

Chapter 5 : Bad Habits, Bad Bank Account 29

Chapter 6 : You Don't Understand Money   33

Chapter 7 : Working Hard But Staying Poor   39

Chapter 8 : Fear of Starting 43

Chapter 9 : The Power of Personal Ownership   47

Chapter 10 : The Comparison Trap 53

Chapter 11 : You Are the Average of Five People   55

Chapter 12 :   Procrastination – The Silent Thief of Time   57

Chapter 13 : The Luck Lie   59

Chapter 14 : You've Been Trained to Stay Broke   61

Chapter 15 : How to Build Wealth from Zero   65

Chapter 16 : The 30-Day Wealth Reset Plan   71

Chapter 17 : Stop Spending Like You're Rich   77

Chapter 18 : How to Stay Rich Once You Get There   83

Chapter 19 : How to Teach Wealth to Your Children   89

Conclusion : 95

Introduction

I never planned on writing a book about poverty.

In fact, for most of my life, I actively tried not to think about money at all. It felt safer that way. Money, after all, was the source of stress, of arguments, of whispered anxieties that floated through my childhood home like ghosts no one wanted to name.

I grew up like many of us do—with parents who worked tirelessly, who sacrificed silently, who did everything "right" yet still found themselves barely staying above water. They weren't irresponsible or reckless; they were just stuck in a pattern they couldn't see clearly enough to escape.

It wasn't until much later—after years of trying to solve money problems by simply working harder—that I started to ask a different question. Instead of wondering, "Why am I broke?" I began asking, "**What if I've been trained to stay broke?**"

This shift in perspective changed everything.

Suddenly, I wasn't looking at a personal failure; I was examining a system. I wasn't just looking at my bank account; I was analyzing my beliefs. I wasn't just trying to earn more; I was finally seeing the invisible forces that had been quietly directing my financial decisions all along.

What I discovered wasn't pleasant—but it was powerful.

I saw clearly how the habits, ideas, and beliefs that had seemed so normal to me were actually perfectly designed to keep me exactly where I was: hardworking yet broke, stressed yet stagnant, ambitious yet stuck.

This book is about sharing what I've learned since that moment.

Because here's the truth I discovered: Being poor isn't just about money. It's not simply about how much you earn or save or invest. Being poor is about the invisible patterns that shape how you think about yourself, your potential, and your possibilities.

These patterns aren't random. They were handed down through generations, reinforced by society, and ingrained so deeply that we rarely stop to question them.

I wrote this book because I want you to stop and question them.

In the pages ahead, you'll find the tools I used—and still use—to rewrite the story of poverty into one of wealth, freedom, and growth. But unlike most financial books, this isn't just a collection of tips and strategies. It's a deeper journey into the roots of why you think and behave the way you do with money.

We'll explore how subtle shifts in your beliefs and habits can create massive changes in your financial life. You'll learn how your environment silently shapes your financial outcomes, why comfort is often the greatest obstacle to wealth, and how excuses that sound intelligent can quietly erode your dreams.

You'll also learn to recognize the hidden scripts you've inherited about money—scripts that may have felt normal, even comforting, but that are quietly robbing you of your true potential.

But this journey isn't just about awareness—it's about action. Each chapter ends with reflective exercises and journal prompts specifically designed to move you from insight to implementation. These aren't just theoretical concepts; they're practical steps I've personally tested, refined, and lived through.

My goal isn't just to teach you how to manage money better; it's to help you become someone who thinks differently about wealth entirely. Because changing your financial life isn't just about changing your actions—it's about changing your identity.

When you see yourself not as someone destined to struggle, but as someone capable of building wealth intentionally, the real transformation begins.

And this transformation matters, not just for you, but for everyone who comes after you. When you rewrite your financial story, you rewrite it for your family, your community, and every generation that follows.

If you've ever felt stuck, frustrated, or confused about why your hard work never seems to pay off, this book is for you. If you've ever wondered why success seems easy for others yet impossible for you, this book is for you. And if you've ever secretly feared that poverty might be your fate, I promise you—it's not.

You weren't born to stay broke. You weren't born to quietly settle. You weren't born to replay the cycles handed down to you.

You were born to rewrite them.

By picking up this book, you've already started. Let's keep going.

Chapter 1
The Poverty Programming

When I was a child, my family never explicitly talked about money, yet it somehow dominated every corner of our lives. It wasn't something that needed words—it was expressed through tense dinners, subtle sighs at the grocery store checkout, and the quiet anxiety that filled the house when bills arrived. Without realizing it, I was learning lessons about money before I even understood what money really was.

I remember distinctly watching my mother sit at the kitchen table, piles of envelopes and papers spread before her. Her brow furrowed as she calculated and recalculated numbers, a constant, silent negotiation between what we needed and what we could afford. This image, repeated month after month, taught me something profound: money was scarce, stressful, and something we didn't control. It was something that controlled us.

Years later, as I began to examine my own complicated relationship with money, I understood that these early experiences had left a permanent mark. It wasn't just about how much money I earned or saved—there was something deeper, more elusive at play. I was operating from what I came to call "poverty programming," an invisible script that dictated my actions and limited my outcomes without me ever consciously choosing it.

This poverty programming isn't just personal; it's universal. Most of us inherit our financial identities from those who raised us, internalizing their beliefs about what is possible, permissible, or even desirable when it comes to money. These beliefs don't come as obvious warnings. They're subtle, wrapped in caution and love, spoken softly but clearly:

"We can't afford that."
"Money doesn't grow on trees."
"Be realistic."
"Rich people aren't like us."

Each of these phrases seems harmless, even wise. Yet each one quietly sets boundaries around your potential. They tell you to stay small, stay safe, and most importantly, stay familiar.

How the Script Forms

You didn't choose your initial money story, but you carry it anyway. It was handed to you before you were old enough to question it. And the moment you accept that story as true, it begins to shape your life.

Maybe your parents taught you that struggle was honorable, that financial stability was something other people achieved. Maybe your neighborhood showed you that wealth was for the "lucky," not the diligent. Maybe your school prepared you for a steady job, never once teaching you how to own assets or build income streams independent of a paycheck.

Whatever the specifics, your poverty programming becomes your default. It quietly, powerfully influences every decision you make about money—from what jobs you think you deserve, to how comfortable you feel charging for your skills, to whether you invest in your future or cling fearfully to every dollar.

These inherited scripts aren't logical; they're emotional. They were passed down through generations, creating a cycle that keeps families trapped—not because they don't want to escape, but because they don't even realize they're trapped in the first place.

Unlearning What You Never Chose

The hardest part of changing your financial reality isn't learning new habits; it's recognizing the old ones you never chose but still follow unconsciously.

When you start questioning these generational patterns, it can feel unsettling—not just to you, but to those around you. People may react defensively, asking:

"Why are you acting different?"
"You think you're better than us now?"
"Money changes people."

They're right, of course. Money does change people—it should. It changes your opportunities, your health, your relationships, and your stress levels. Money changes your ability to say yes to what you truly want and no to what you no longer tolerate.

You don't owe anyone your continued struggle, not even your family. You don't owe your ancestors another generation of survival. Instead, you owe them—and yourself—a new legacy: a reprogrammed lineage where your children grow up equipped with financial literacy instead of financial anxiety, confidence instead of caution, abundance instead of scarcity.

This is your new responsibility: not just to break patterns, but to create new ones intentionally.

Awareness is the First Rebellion

Changing your financial life isn't just about getting smarter with your money. It's about reclaiming your story and your power. The moment you become aware of your poverty programming, something remarkable happens: its grip weakens. You move from automatic responses to conscious choices.

You start noticing your habits. You start questioning old beliefs. You start rewriting scripts that no longer serve you.

Instead of saying, "I can't afford that," you begin to ask, "How can I afford that?"
Instead of declaring, "I'm just bad with money," you start affirming, "I'm learning how to build wealth every day."

These shifts might seem small—but they're seismic. Because the moment you begin to believe something different about yourself, your behaviors align to prove it true.

Creating Your New Money Identity

You can't erase your old scripts overnight. But you can overwrite them gradually by consciously crafting new beliefs and repeatedly acting in alignment with them.

This isn't a comfortable process, and it's rarely quiet. It demands that you confront your own biases, your family's assumptions, and your culture's norms. But as you do, each small change creates a ripple, spreading outward to reshape your reality.

Your new money identity starts with small wins: saving your first $50, investing your first dollar, saying "no" to expenses that don't align with your goals. Each decision strengthens your new identity and weakens the old script.

You're not becoming someone different—you're becoming more authentically yourself, free from inherited limitations.

Reflection

Take a moment now—not just to read, but to reflect and rewrite.

What money beliefs were passed down to you—directly or indirectly?
Think about common phrases, emotional responses, or attitudes toward money you observed in childhood.

What beliefs about money have you absorbed from your environment?
Who around you succeeded financially? Who struggled? How did these examples shape your idea of "normal"?

How do you speak to yourself about money now?
Do you find yourself repeating limiting phrases or self-judgments?

Chapter 2
Comfort Is Killing You

Several years ago, I met a friend named Adam who embodied what most people would describe as stability. He had a steady job, a decent apartment, and a predictable schedule. Every morning, he followed the same routine: wake up, grab coffee from the same shop, commute to work the same way, and come home to the same TV shows and meals each night.

From the outside, it looked comfortable—maybe even enviable. But beneath that comforting routine, something was slowly happening: Adam was growing numb.

It wasn't immediately obvious. It wasn't dramatic. It was quiet, slow, subtle, and deeply dangerous.

Adam had dreams, just like everyone else. He'd talk enthusiastically about starting his own business, traveling, learning new skills, and finally taking the leap to do something meaningful with his life.

But as soon as the conversation ended, the excitement would fade into excuses:

"Maybe next year."
"When things calm down."
"I just need more time."

Years passed, and Adam's dreams never came any closer.

They simply hovered in the background, familiar and reassuring, never daring to move toward reality. Why? Because comfort had quietly replaced ambition. Comfort had become his prison.

And Adam is not alone.

Why Comfort Feels So Dangerous

Comfort is tricky because it masquerades as success. It feels stable, safe, and reliable. But what it really does is keep you right where you are—comfortable, but not growing.

Comfort tells you to hold onto the familiar, even if the familiar isn't fulfilling. It convinces you that stepping into uncertainty is foolish. It whispers that it's safer to stay quietly disappointed than to risk loudly failing.

Comfort, ironically, becomes your greatest source of discomfort—the discomfort of knowing you're living far beneath your potential.

Think of comfort as an emotional anesthetic: it dulls your senses, quiets your dreams, and numbs you to possibilities. Before long, your goals seem less urgent, your dreams less important, and your future more distant.

Comfort doesn't shout. It gently whispers, "Not now. Maybe later." And later never comes.

The True Cost of "Playing It Safe"

Most people who choose comfort never calculate its true cost. They don't measure the opportunities missed, the potential never realized, or the life left unlived. Comfort quietly steals these possibilities day after day, year after year.

Maybe you recognize yourself in Adam's story. Maybe your comfort zone looks like a job you dislike but tolerate because it pays the bills. Maybe it's the business idea you haven't launched because you're afraid to fail. Perhaps it's a relationship that no longer fulfills you, but feels safer than the unknown.

These comfortable choices may not hurt immediately. But their cumulative impact is devastating. Every day spent avoiding discomfort is a day spent trading your potential for predictability. And predictability is expensive—it costs you your dreams, your growth, and eventually, your self-respect.

Comfort's Greatest Illusion: The Right Time

Perhaps the most dangerous comfort illusion is believing there's a "right time" to change your life.

I hear it constantly:

"I'll start saving when I earn more."
"I'll build the business when things settle down."
"I'll chase my dreams when I feel ready."

But here's the harsh truth: **comfort will never tell you you're ready.**

Ready doesn't exist. The "right time" never comes. If you're waiting for comfort to signal when to act, you'll wait forever.

Action—especially uncomfortable action—must be chosen deliberately, consciously, repeatedly. It rarely feels perfect, it seldom feels safe, but it always moves you forward.

Breaking Free of the Comfort Trap

You can't reason your way out of comfort; you must act your way out. Comfort, by definition, feels good. Change, by definition, does not—at least not at first.

But here's the good news: discomfort fades faster than regret. Yes, the first step toward change might feel risky, awkward, or frightening, but discomfort is temporary. The pain of regret—of dreams unlived and potential unexplored—is permanent.

Start with small acts of discomfort:

- [ ] Speak up about your ideas, even when you're nervous.
- [ ] Launch your side hustle before you feel ready.
- [ ] Invest small amounts regularly, even if it feels awkward.
- [ ] Set boundaries in relationships, even if it feels unfamiliar.

With each small uncomfortable choice, your comfort zone expands. Each action builds courage, momentum, and confidence—until discomfort itself becomes familiar and empowering.

Eventually, you'll realize something powerful: comfort was never keeping you safe—it was keeping you small.

Comfort Is a Choice. Growth Is a Decision.

Today, right now, you face a decision: comfort or growth?

Comfort is seductive. It promises ease, predictability, and familiarity. But growth offers you something infinitely more valuable—progress, meaning, and fulfillment.

Remember Adam? He eventually did something bold: he quit his stable job and took a risk on his business. It wasn't easy, and it definitely wasn't comfortable. But the moment he embraced discomfort, he began living a life of his own design, not one dictated by habit or fear.

You have that same choice. Comfort will always whisper, "Stay here; you're safe." Growth will always challenge you to step forward, even if your next move feels uncertain or scary.

Choose carefully. One path is predictable—but limited. The other is uncertain—but limitless.

Reflection

Comfort has a cost, but change starts with clarity. Reflect honestly and deeply:

1. **What part of your life feels comfortable but isn't fulfilling?**
   Identify what feels "safe" yet quietly unsatisfying—your job, your relationships, your daily routine.

2. **What fear is hiding behind your comfort?**
   Are you afraid of failing, judgment, disappointment, or uncertainty?

3. **What small uncomfortable step can you take this week to break your comfort pattern?**
   Make it practical and immediate. What action will you commit to right now?

Chapter 3
Excuses That Keep You Broke

When I first met Nathan, he was full of potential. Smart, talented, and hardworking, Nathan was the kind of person you'd confidently bet would achieve great things. He was filled with ideas, dreams, and ambitions. He talked passionately about starting a business, investing, traveling, and living a life that reflected his true capabilities.

Yet year after year, his plans remained just that—plans. They never translated into reality. Whenever we talked about his goals, Nathan would give the same familiar responses:

"I just need more time to plan."
"The market isn't right yet."
"I'll do it when I have more savings."

On the surface, these reasons sounded logical, even prudent. But the deeper truth was painfully obvious: they were excuses, carefully disguised as intelligent caution. Nathan wasn't lazy—far from it. He was simply afraid. Afraid of failure, afraid of judgment, afraid of what might happen if he actually took a chance.

Nathan's story isn't unique; in fact, it's deeply common. Many of us unknowingly sabotage our dreams through excuses that seem reasonable. But over time, those seemingly intelligent delays quietly erode our potential and keep us trapped in financial stagnation.

The Intelligent Excuse Trap

Excuses are fascinating because they're incredibly convincing. They don't sound like weaknesses or delays. Instead, they masquerade as rational planning, thoughtful hesitation, or prudent caution. Excuses are so persuasive precisely because they sound wise.

- "I'll start investing when the economy improves."
- "I'll launch my business once my website looks perfect."
- "I'll begin saving when I earn just a bit more."

Each of these statements is understandable. They're rational. Yet, beneath their logic is something far more dangerous: fear. Fear of embarrassment. Fear of uncertainty. Fear of responsibility.

But here's the truth these excuses hide: there's no perfect moment. There's no perfect economy, no perfect savings number, no perfect website. Waiting for perfect conditions isn't wisdom—it's procrastination.

The Cost of Waiting

What most people don't realize is that excuses aren't free. They come at an enormous cost. Every month spent waiting to invest is another month without compounding interest. Every year spent "perfecting" your business idea is another year without customers, revenue, or growth. Every delay in saving, building, or learning isn't just lost time—it's lost potential.

Nathan, who once dreamed vividly, was losing more than opportunities. He was losing his self-confidence. Every time he delayed, his belief in himself faded a little more. Excuses have a compounding effect, just like investments. Unfortunately, instead of compounding returns, they compound doubt and stagnation.

We rarely measure the cost of not acting. Yet, the price of hesitation—of letting our excuses rule—is far greater than the temporary discomfort of action.

Fear Disguised as Logic

Excuses are essentially fears disguised as reasons. Every "logical" explanation for delay has an emotional root.

Think of the last thing you postponed—launching your business, investing, creating something meaningful. What excuse did you give yourself? Was it time, money, readiness?

Now ask yourself honestly: was it truly about those things, or was it about fear? Fear of judgment, fear of failure, fear of success itself?

Facing this truth isn't easy, but it's essential. When we recognize excuses for what they truly are—fear dressed in logic—we regain the power to act. Awareness is the first step towards reclaiming control of your financial future.

The Smallest Action Beats the Best Excuse

Years after our first conversation, Nathan finally made one small move—he registered his business. This simple, inexpensive, and quick action broke through years of inertia. Suddenly, what had felt impossible was now real. He hadn't just talked about his dream—he had claimed it.

Taking action doesn't need to be dramatic. In fact, the smaller the better. Small actions dismantle excuses because they require minimal risk. Each small act moves you from thinking about your goals to actively pursuing them.

You don't need the perfect business plan—just post one offer online. You don't need a large investment—just invest a small amount today. You don't need a perfect savings strategy—just automate $10 per paycheck.

These actions seem insignificant at first. But each small step creates momentum, and momentum, over time, crushes excuses. It transforms vague dreams into tangible reality.

Choosing Responsibility Over Excuses

The difference between people who achieve their financial goals and those who stay stuck isn't intelligence or talent—it's responsibility.

Excuses shift responsibility away from you. They let you off the hook temporarily, but they also keep you trapped permanently. Taking responsibility feels uncomfortable because it means risking failure, rejection, and uncertainty. Yet, it's also the most liberating choice you can make. It puts you back in charge of your life.

Taking responsibility means choosing imperfect action over perfect inaction. It means saying, "Even though I'm afraid, I'll move forward anyway." Responsibility transforms your identity from someone who dreams to someone who acts. It turns you from a victim of circumstance into a creator of outcomes.

Nathan learned this firsthand. Today, he's thriving. His business isn't perfect—but it exists. He isn't fearless—but he's brave enough to keep moving forward. Nathan traded excuses for responsibility, and his life has been forever transformed.

Your financial future is waiting for you to make the same choice.

Reflection

This chapter's insights matter most when they're applied. Reflect honestly, deeply, and intentionally:

1. **What's your go-to excuse for delaying important financial actions?**
   Name it clearly—time, readiness, money, perfection?

2. **What fear is hiding behind that excuse?**
   Fear of failure, rejection, embarrassment, or success?

3. **What's one small, immediate action you can take to challenge this excuse today?**
   Small actions carry immense power. What simple step can you commit to?

Chapter 4

Your Environment Is Poison

For years, my friend Jamal dreamed of starting his own design firm. He had a sharp eye, a knack for aesthetics, and a passion for creative work. He knew exactly what he wanted—to build something that represented him, to express his creativity, to have real ownership over his life.

But whenever he began moving toward his goal, something always seemed to stop him. It wasn't lack of skill or opportunity—it was his environment.

Jamal's closest friends constantly complained about their jobs, mocked ambition, and treated dreams as childish fantasies. Whenever Jamal spoke about his business ideas, they laughed:

"You're dreaming, man."
"Be realistic."
"People like us don't build businesses—we work."

At first, Jamal brushed off these comments. After all, they were his friends. He'd known them since childhood. But slowly, subtly, their negativity began shaping his thoughts. Eventually, he began believing what he heard. His excitement dimmed. His plans stalled. Jamal didn't realize his environment had poisoned his dreams until years later, when he saw someone else build the exact business he'd once imagined.

He learned a painful truth: **your environment quietly shapes your identity, your decisions, and ultimately your destiny.**

You Become Your Surroundings

You are shaped by the voices you hear most frequently. They mold your beliefs, influence your expectations, and set your standards.

If your closest circle routinely avoids risk, mocks ambition, and settles for mediocrity, you'll inevitably follow their lead. You'll shrink your goals to match theirs, lower your standards to blend in, and suppress your ambitions to avoid standing out.

But environments can also work in the opposite direction. Surround yourself with builders, creators, and optimists, and suddenly, your goals seem achievable—even inevitable. Positive environments normalize success, growth, and wealth. Negative environments normalize stagnation, skepticism, and scarcity.

Your environment isn't neutral. It's either pulling you toward your goals or dragging you away from them.

The Hidden Power of Proximity

It's not just your social circle that shapes you—your physical surroundings quietly influence your financial choices too.

Imagine you're trying to save money. You know it's important, you have clear goals, yet you consistently overspend. Why? Maybe your environment is set up for spending rather than saving.

The stores you visit, the websites you browse, the notifications you receive, even your social media feeds—all are designed to encourage spending. Without realizing it, your surroundings have been structured to promote habits that drain your wallet.

But small changes in your physical environment can dramatically shift your financial behaviors. If you keep impulse purchases out of reach, you'll buy fewer. If you automate savings so they happen effortlessly, you'll save more. Your environment doesn't just shape your actions—it shapes your default behaviors.

Toxic Environments Quietly Limit Potential

Toxic environments rarely announce themselves. They're subtle, often comfortable. They rarely feel overtly dangerous, yet they're quietly lethal to your potential.

They show up as friends who discourage rather than uplift. They appear as family members who undermine rather than support. They manifest in workplaces that reward conformity rather than creativity. The toxicity often feels normal simply because it's familiar.

But here's the truth: just because it feels familiar doesn't mean it's safe. Familiarity is comfort—not clarity. You may not even notice the poison because you've grown immune to it. Yet, slowly but surely, it seeps into your identity, sabotaging your confidence, your dreams, and ultimately your wealth.

Curating Your New Environment

Changing your environment doesn't necessarily mean abandoning your friends or family overnight. Instead, it's about intentionally curating new inputs—inputs aligned with the person you want to become, rather than the person you've been.

Start by surrounding yourself with voices of growth:

- Join online communities filled with ambitious, positive people.
- Listen to podcasts and audiobooks from those who've built the financial life you desire.
- Spend time in spaces that inspire and encourage your growth.

Next, intentionally adjust your physical surroundings:

- Automate savings so your environment naturally supports your financial goals.
- Keep reminders of your financial goals visible—your fridge, mirror, screensaver.
- Limit exposure to environments (physical or digital) that trigger spending or negative patterns.

These small shifts gradually but powerfully realign your environment to reflect your ambitions, rather than sabotage them.

Choosing a Better Circle

One of the most critical—and often uncomfortable—decisions you'll make is choosing your social circle.

When Jamal finally acknowledged his environment's toxicity, he made the hard decision to distance himself from negative influences. It was uncomfortable. At first, he felt lonely. But slowly, he connected with new people—mentors, entrepreneurs, creatives. They didn't mock his dreams; they amplified them. They showed him what was possible.

Suddenly, Jamal's beliefs shifted. He wasn't fighting his environment anymore. He was being carried by it. Within a year, he had launched his design firm, and his life changed dramatically.

You don't need perfect conditions. You just need a circle that believes growth is normal, ambition is admirable, and dreams are achievable.

Your Environment Reflects Your Future

Your environment today predicts your future tomorrow. Change your environment, and you change the trajectory of your life. It's not instant—but it's inevitable.

Today, take a hard look at your surroundings. Who do you listen to? What voices influence your choices? Are they pushing you forward or pulling you back?

You have the power to curate your environment intentionally. You decide the voices you hear, the habits you adopt, and the beliefs you accept. Every choice you make about your environment is a vote for the future you're building.

Don't underestimate the silent power of your surroundings. Because ultimately, your environment doesn't just shape your life—it determines who you become.

Reflection

Reflection transforms insight into action. Take a moment and reflect deeply:

1. **Who in your current environment is holding you back rather than lifting you up?**
   Be honest and clear about who supports your growth and who limits it.

2. **What's one toxic habit or environment you consistently find yourself in?**
   How does it quietly sabotage your financial and personal goals?

3. **What immediate change can you make today to create a more supportive environment?**
   Think practically—joining a community, automating a financial habit, or limiting a toxic relationship.

Chapter 5
Bad Habits, Bad Bank Account

Early in my twenties, I had a friend named Sara. Like many young adults, Sara dreamed of financial freedom and stability. She imagined herself traveling, investing, and building wealth for her future. But reality consistently fell short of her dreams.

Sara was smart, ambitious, and had a good job. On paper, she had everything she needed to thrive financially. Yet month after month, her bank account painted a different story—one of struggle, overdraft fees, and frustration. She couldn't understand why financial success eluded her despite her efforts.

One afternoon, Sara and I sat down to examine her spending. At first glance, everything seemed reasonable. But looking closer, we noticed subtle patterns—daily habits—that quietly drained her resources: expensive coffees every morning, frequent spontaneous online purchases, dinners out several times a week, and a subscription list that seemed endless.

These habits individually felt insignificant, harmless even. But together, they formed a powerful drain on Sara's finances. She had no dramatic spending addictions, just a series of small, unexamined habits quietly sabotaging her financial goals.

Sara's story isn't unusual. In fact, most people struggle financially not because of major mistakes, but due to small, consistent patterns. It's rarely one big decision that keeps people broke—it's countless small, unnoticed ones.

Your Habits Shape Your Financial Future

Habits define your life more than you realize. They operate quietly in the background, influencing every decision, action, and outcome you experience. Each habit is like a tiny vote cast every day—for your success or your struggle.

Consider your daily routines. Maybe, like Sara, you buy coffee daily, shop impulsively when bored, or avoid checking your bank balance because it feels stressful. Individually, these actions may seem trivial, but cumulatively, they become a powerful financial force—shaping your bank account, your stress levels, and your future.

Habits aren't neutral. They either move you toward financial freedom or deeper into financial struggle.

Why Small Habits Matter Most

Many people underestimate small habits, mistakenly believing wealth is built from dramatic actions: winning the lottery, inheriting money, or landing a massive business deal. But real wealth-building is rarely so glamorous. It's built quietly, methodically, habitually.

Think of habits as small financial leaks or investments. Every unnecessary expense, no matter how minor, drains resources you could otherwise invest. Conversely, every small savings habit compounds over time into meaningful wealth.

Sara's daily $6 coffee habit didn't seem extravagant—until we calculated its true cost: nearly $2,200 a year. Over ten years, invested at even modest returns, it could have grown into tens of thousands of dollars. Suddenly, a small habit felt very large.

Your life—financially and personally—is shaped more by your daily patterns than by occasional dramatic efforts. The secret to wealth isn't extraordinary action—it's ordinary consistency.

Identity and Habits: The Hidden Connection

Your habits aren't just random actions; they reflect your identity. If you see yourself as someone who struggles financially, your habits will mirror that belief. You'll spend impulsively, avoid budgeting, or sabotage savings without realizing it—because your actions reflect your subconscious identity.

On the other hand, when you shift your identity from someone who's "bad with money" to someone who "builds wealth intentionally," your habits follow. You become deliberate, mindful, and strategic. You start small, but your new identity reinforces positive behaviors until they become automatic.

Habits aren't merely about actions—they're about who you believe you are. To change your finances, you must first change your identity.

Replacing Bad Habits, Not Just Removing Them

Habits are deeply ingrained because they fulfill emotional needs. You don't spend impulsively because you're irresponsible—you do it because you're bored, stressed, or seeking comfort. If you simply try to stop these habits without replacing them, you'll inevitably fall back into old patterns.

The solution isn't simply removing bad habits—it's actively replacing them. Instead of shopping to relieve boredom, you might read, exercise, or learn a new skill. Instead of avoiding your finances, you could establish a habit of reviewing your accounts weekly, transforming stress into clarity.

Sara began replacing her costly habits intentionally. Instead of daily coffees, she invested in a high-quality coffee maker. Instead of impulsive online shopping, she set up automatic investments into her savings account. She didn't eliminate her desires; she redirected them toward actions that built her financial future rather than drained it.

Consistency Over Perfection

The goal isn't perfect financial habits—it's consistency. Wealth-building habits don't need to be flawless; they just need to be repeated frequently enough to create meaningful change.

Small, consistent habits have a compounding effect. Sara didn't overhaul her entire financial life overnight. She simply committed to small, consistent actions—automatically saving $20 each week, reviewing her budget monthly, and investing small amounts regularly.

Over months, these small actions created big results. She paid off debts, saved significantly more, and finally felt in control of her finances. Sara learned that consistency always beats perfection.

Your Habits Are a Choice

Your habits—positive or negative—are not fixed. They're choices. Every habit you have today was once deliberately or unconsciously chosen, and every habit you adopt tomorrow will shape your financial future.

You have the power to choose differently. You can choose habits aligned with your dreams rather than your fears. You can build routines that reinforce your desired identity rather than undermine it. Every new habit is a vote for the future you want—not the past you inherited.

Financial transformation isn't about making perfect decisions occasionally. It's about making better decisions consistently, every single day.

Reflection

Transformation happens through reflection followed by action. Take a moment now and reflect honestly:

1. **What small daily habits quietly drain your financial resources?**
   Be specific—morning coffee, impulse purchases, unused subscriptions.

2. **What emotional needs are these habits meeting?**
   Are they relieving stress, boredom, loneliness, or something else?

3. **What positive financial habit could you replace this week to meet that emotional need more constructively?**
   Think practically: automate savings, track spending, replace shopping with another activity.

Chapter 6
You Don't Understand Money

I once met a man named Alex, who by all outward appearances had a successful life. He earned a good income, drove a nice car, and seemed financially secure. But behind this polished facade, Alex lived in constant anxiety about money. Each paycheck brought relief—but only briefly. Soon enough, stress returned, bills piled up, and confusion reigned. He couldn't figure out why he never seemed to get ahead despite earning more than most people.

One evening, frustrated and desperate, Alex asked me, "Why does money feel so impossible to control?"

The answer, I explained, wasn't lack of effort—it was lack of understanding. Like many people, Alex had never truly learned how money works. He had mistaken earning a good salary for financial security, unaware that income alone isn't wealth. He believed hard work automatically translated into financial success, not realizing he was missing essential knowledge about how money actually operates.

Alex's story is remarkably common. Most people grow up without formal financial education. School teaches us history, math, and science, but rarely how to manage, grow, or leverage money. As a result, we make emotional, rather than informed, decisions. We confuse high income with financial security, spend impulsively, and avoid the discomfort of looking closely at our finances.

This lack of understanding isn't just inconvenient—it's financially crippling.

Money Is More Emotional Than Logical

For most people, money isn't simply about numbers; it's deeply emotional. We associate it with security, success, shame, anxiety, or status. These emotions often cloud our judgment, causing irrational decisions that quietly sabotage our goals.

Consider impulse spending. You don't overspend because you're careless or foolish; you overspend because you're bored, stressed, or unhappy. Money becomes a temporary emotional solution rather than a strategic tool. Without understanding your emotions around money, you become trapped in a cycle of financial struggle—earning, spending, worrying, repeating.

Money must be understood logically—not emotionally—to master it. But to shift from emotional reactions to informed choices, you first need to understand how money truly works.

Cash Flow Matters More Than Income

Like Alex, most people believe that earning more is the answer to their financial problems. But increasing your income without understanding cash flow rarely leads to wealth.

Imagine two people: Maria earns $50,000 per year but consistently saves and invests. John earns $120,000 annually but spends nearly everything he makes. Despite earning more than double, John constantly feels broke. His income isn't his issue—it's his cash flow.

Cash flow is simply the relationship between your income and your expenses. Wealthy people aren't necessarily those who earn the most; they're those who manage their cash flow effectively. They spend less than they earn, consistently save, and systematically invest. Even a modest income, managed strategically, can lead to financial freedom over time.

To build wealth, you must understand that it's not about how much money you make—it's about how much money you keep, protect, and multiply.

Assets vs. Liabilities: The Real Secret

The most important financial lesson most people never learn is the difference between assets and liabilities. Without this knowledge, people unknowingly sabotage their financial future.

An asset is something that puts money in your pocket—investments, real estate, or businesses. A liability takes money out of your pocket—expensive cars, credit card debts, or consumer purchases.

Most people spend their lives accumulating liabilities, mistaking them for assets. They buy things that feel like investments—a nice car, designer clothes, expensive gadgets. These things might impress others temporarily, but they quietly drain your financial resources.

Real wealth-building is about accumulating true assets—things that generate income, appreciate in value, or help you multiply your resources. Understanding and acting upon this simple truth will transform your financial future.

Compound Interest: The Invisible Power

Another misunderstood financial principle is compound interest. Albert Einstein famously called compound interest the "eighth wonder of the world." Yet most people never fully grasp its power.

Compound interest simply means that your money earns money, which then earns even more money, multiplying exponentially over time. Small, consistent investments can grow dramatically given enough time and discipline.

For example, saving just $10 daily invested at average returns can become over $400,000 after 30 years. Understanding compound interest isn't about mathematics—it's about appreciating that small, consistent actions yield incredible results when given time. It's the foundational principle of building wealth, yet it remains widely misunderstood and underused.

The High Cost of Financial Avoidance

Many people avoid understanding their finances because it feels overwhelming or stressful. Alex admitted he rarely checked his bank statements, ignored bills, and avoided financial planning because it made him anxious.

But financial avoidance doesn't protect you—it keeps you powerless. What you don't understand controls you. Avoiding financial reality creates anxiety and uncertainty, leaving you vulnerable to emergencies, market shifts, or personal setbacks.

Facing financial truths directly isn't comfortable initially, but clarity is empowering. Once Alex faced his finances honestly, creating a clear budget, investing regularly, and actively tracking cash flow, his anxiety diminished. He finally felt in control—not because his situation magically improved overnight, but because he understood clearly where he stood and how to move forward.

Learning Financial Skills Is Your Responsibility

Financial understanding isn't a luxury—it's a necessity. You cannot build wealth by accident or hope. You must intentionally educate yourself about money, continuously expanding your understanding of how it truly works.

Start simply: track your spending, learn the basics of investing, and understand cash flow. Listen to podcasts, read books, and engage actively with your finances. Financial literacy doesn't require brilliance, only consistent curiosity and commitment.

When you understand money clearly, you transform it from a source of stress into a tool for growth. Clarity is power—and financial clarity is financial freedom.

Reflection

Financial transformation requires reflection followed by action. Take a moment to honestly reflect:

1. **What part of your finances feels overwhelming or unclear?** Identify specifically what you avoid—budgeting, investing, debt management?

2. **How does emotional decision-making affect your finances?** Consider impulse spending, fear of investing, or avoidance habits.

3. **What specific financial concept—cash flow, assets vs. liabilities, compound interest—could you learn about this week to gain clarity?**

WORKING HARD
BUT STAYING POOR

Chapter 7
Working Hard But Staying Poor

My friend Amina was one of the hardest-working people I've ever known. She woke early each morning, stayed late at work, and constantly took on extra shifts. On weekends, she pursued freelance projects and side hustles, sacrificing rest and time with her family to squeeze in additional hours. She was reliable, dedicated, and relentless.

Yet, despite this tireless effort, Amina constantly struggled financially. She barely managed to pay her bills, carried heavy debt, and lived paycheck to paycheck. No matter how many extra hours she worked, the financial freedom she dreamed about remained frustratingly out of reach.

One evening, exhausted and disheartened, Amina asked me the question she'd been silently wrestling with for years:

"Why do I work so hard and still feel broke?"

Her pain was obvious—and familiar. Millions of people share Amina's struggle, believing that working harder is the key to financial freedom. But as she learned, hard work alone rarely creates wealth. In fact, many of the hardest-working people remain financially trapped, never understanding why effort doesn't translate into prosperity.

The problem isn't effort—it's the misunderstanding of how money and effort truly interact.

Why Hard Work Alone Isn't Enough

We've all heard the advice: "Work hard, and success will follow." While hard work is valuable, it's incomplete advice. If it were true, construction workers, teachers, and frontline workers—some of the hardest-working individuals—would be among the wealthiest. Yet they often struggle financially.

Amina was trapped in a common misconception: believing that effort automatically equates to wealth. But hard work without leverage, strategy, or ownership simply leads to exhaustion, not freedom. If you're only trading your hours for dollars, your earning potential is inherently limited—no matter how diligently you work.

Real wealth-building isn't about trading more time—it's about learning to use your time differently.

Trading Time for Money: The Hidden Trap

When your primary method of earning is trading time for money, you're trapped in a cycle of constant effort with limited reward. You can't scale time—you have only 24 hours in a day. Every hour you sell to someone else is an hour you can't use to build something of your own.

Amina's situation illustrated this painfully. Her constant extra hours increased her income temporarily, but they didn't create lasting wealth. Instead, they created burnout, stress, and limited growth. The harder she worked at hourly tasks, the more financially stuck she became, unable to leverage her effort into sustainable progress.

Trading time for money isn't inherently bad—it's simply insufficient. To build wealth, you must learn to leverage your effort beyond hourly income.

Ownership Changes the Game

Wealth is built through ownership—not just effort. Consider this scenario: Two people work equally hard. One works hourly for someone else, while the other builds a business, creates products, or invests in assets. Over time, who accumulates wealth?

The answer is obvious: the one who owns something.

Ownership allows your effort to multiply. When you build a business, create content, develop a product, or invest in assets, your efforts compound over time. Your income grows independent of how many hours you physically work. You're no longer solely dependent on trading time—you're leveraging it.

Imagine Amina creating a simple digital course about her freelance skills instead of working additional hourly shifts. Initially, the effort feels similar. But once created, her course continues earning income without her constant presence. She's created leverage—and leverage, not raw effort, builds wealth.

Why Loyalty to a Paycheck Can Hurt You

Another barrier to financial growth is emotional loyalty to a steady paycheck. Stability feels safe. We're conditioned from childhood to seek secure employment, avoid risks, and stay grateful for whatever income we have—even if it keeps us stuck.

But stability without growth is quietly dangerous. It convinces you to accept financial stagnation. You become loyal to comfort, quietly tolerating being underpaid, overlooked, or undervalued because "at least it's safe."

Amina had fallen into this exact trap. She feared leaving her stable job because it provided predictable income. Yet that predictable income wasn't enough to escape financial stress. Her loyalty, rather than protecting her, trapped her in perpetual scarcity.

Wealth requires courage—the courage to seek growth over safety, opportunity over certainty, and ownership over mere employment.

Leverage Effort, Not Just Increase It

The key isn't simply working harder—it's working smarter. Real wealth comes from leveraging effort, not endlessly expanding it.

For Amina, this meant shifting her focus. Instead of pouring more hours into hourly tasks, she redirected some of her effort into building assets. She created digital products, started investing small amounts consistently, and automated savings into investments. Initially, progress felt slow—but leverage builds exponentially.

Within months, Amina saw her income sources diversify. She earned income without constant extra hours, providing breathing room, confidence, and control. Her effort was finally working for her, rather than exhausting her.

Your goal isn't just to work harder—it's to ensure your hard work compounds into wealth through ownership, assets, and systems.

Breaking the Hard Work Myth

Working hard isn't a virtue if it keeps you poor. Real success isn't about relentless effort—it's about strategic effort. When you understand leverage and ownership, your hard work finally pays off meaningfully.

Amina's story didn't just change financially; it changed personally. She regained energy, time, and confidence. Hard work no longer trapped her; it empowered her. She understood clearly that the key to escaping financial struggle wasn't working harder—it was working smarter, leveraging effort into ownership.

Hard work without leverage leads to struggle. Hard work with leverage leads to wealth.

The choice isn't about working harder—it's about working differently.

Reflection

Take a moment to deeply reflect. Changing your financial future starts here:

1. **Where in your life are you trapped trading time for money without leverage?**
   Identify areas where your effort isn't scalable or sustainable.

2. **What emotional loyalties keep you stuck financially?**
   Are you overly loyal to a steady job or reluctant to risk growth?

3. **What's one small, specific step you can take today to build ownership or leverage your effort?**
   Consider creating a small product, automating investments, or exploring a scalable skill.

Chapter 8
Fear of Starting

Years ago, I met a talented young woman named Fatima, whose dreams were vibrant and ambitious. She envisioned opening her own bakery—a cozy place filled with warmth, laughter, and irresistible aromas. Fatima spent countless hours meticulously planning recipes, sketching designs, and envisioning exactly how her dream bakery would look and feel.

Yet, month after month, year after year, Fatima remained stuck. She never actually opened her bakery. Despite her detailed planning, research, and preparations, she never moved beyond dreaming. Each time she prepared to start, something held her back.

One evening, exhausted and frustrated, she admitted to me:

"I know exactly what I want—but I'm terrified to actually start. What if it fails?"

Fatima's fear is painfully familiar. Most of us know the fear of starting well—the paralyzing anxiety about taking the first step. It disguises itself as rational caution, careful preparation, or thoughtful hesitation. But behind this mask is always the same quiet fear: *What if I fail? What if I'm not good enough?*

This fear doesn't just delay your dreams—it kills them quietly, slowly, and permanently.

Why the First Step Feels Impossible

Starting something new feels dangerous because it means risking failure. It means leaving the comfortable safety of imagination and stepping into the uncertain reality of action.

For Fatima, opening the bakery meant risking financial failure, judgment from others, and painful disappointment. Staying in the planning phase allowed her to feel safe and in control, enjoying the comfort of her dream without facing the reality of possible failure.

Many people, like Fatima, find the first step impossible not because they're unprepared, but because stepping forward means giving up the comforting safety of "potential." It means trading possibility for vulnerability, fantasy for feedback.

But the longer you delay starting, the harder that first step becomes. The more time spent dreaming rather than doing, the heavier and scarier action becomes.

Perfection Is Just Fear in Disguise

Another common excuse that stops people from starting is perfectionism. Fatima's bakery was ready on paper long before she felt "ready" to start. She endlessly refined recipes, redesigned menus, and restructured business plans—not to improve them, but to delay the moment of vulnerability.

Perfectionism feels noble. It appears responsible, even admirable. But perfectionism is really just fear dressed up as diligence. It gives us permission to avoid action while pretending we're preparing thoughtfully. In reality, perfectionism simply delays—and often prevents—the crucial first step.

You don't need perfect conditions to start. You need courage to act imperfectly and refine as you go. Clarity doesn't come before action—it emerges through action.

The Magic of Small Beginnings

Fatima eventually realized the truth: starting doesn't have to mean starting big. The myth of a perfect, grand opening had held her back for years. Real progress begins much smaller and simpler.

She decided to start by baking at home and offering free samples to friends. It wasn't grand or perfect, but it was real. The simple act of baking those first pastries broke through years of hesitation. It transformed her from someone who dreamed about baking into someone who baked. This subtle but powerful shift gave her courage, momentum, and clarity.

Small beginnings have magic. They remove pressure and expectations, transforming intimidating goals into achievable actions. You don't need a perfect business plan—just one small action to move forward.

Action Kills Fear

The moment Fatima took her first action, fear began losing its power. Action, even tiny, imperfect action, is the ultimate fear-killer. Fear thrives in stillness, uncertainty, and avoidance. Action breaks fear's grip by shifting your energy from worry to work.

With every small step—baking samples, posting photos online, getting feedback—Fatima's fear shrank, replaced by confidence and excitement. Action transformed her fear from an insurmountable obstacle into manageable anxiety.

You don't need to conquer fear before starting—you simply need to start despite fear. Each action weakens fear's control, building courage, clarity, and momentum.

You Are the Permission You Seek

Most people wait for permission to start. They wait for validation, approval, or some external sign that they're finally ready. Fatima had waited years, hoping someone or something would confirm she was qualified, capable, or prepared enough.

But here's the truth: No external permission will ever feel sufficient. The approval you seek must come from yourself. Starting isn't about readiness—it's about choosing to move forward despite uncertainty.

Fatima eventually understood this. She realized that she didn't need external permission—she simply needed to give herself permission to start. The day she began baking in her own kitchen, she stopped waiting for permission and took responsibility instead. From that moment, everything changed.

You don't need perfect conditions, approval, or validation. You simply need to decide you're worthy of your own permission—and begin.

Your Dreams Deserve Action

Fatima's bakery is now thriving. It wasn't easy or instant, but each step she took reinforced her courage, clarity, and capabilities. Her life transformed not through endless preparation, but through deliberate action.

Your dreams deserve the same courage. Whatever your goal—launching a business, investing, saving money, creating a side income—start now, even imperfectly. Take one small action today, then another tomorrow.

Your dreams are worth more than fear, perfectionism, or hesitation. Starting isn't about having perfect conditions—it's about having enough courage to act despite uncertainty. It's about understanding that your first step doesn't have to be perfect; it simply needs to be taken.

The fear of starting is real, but action makes fear manageable. Every small step forward weakens fear's grip, strengthening your confidence, clarity, and courage. Give yourself permission to begin. Your dreams are waiting.

Chapter Reflection & Journal: Overcoming Fear

Reflection followed by action transforms dreams into reality. Take a moment now and honestly reflect:

1. **What goal or dream have you been avoiding out of fear of starting?**
   Name clearly what you've postponed repeatedly.

2. **What specific fears or perfectionist tendencies have stopped you from taking action?**
   Be honest—fear of failure, judgment, vulnerability?

3. **What small, imperfect action can you commit to taking today or this week?**
   Start as small and simple as possible.

Chapter 9
The Power of Personal Ownership

Early in my career, I met a man named Yusuf who taught me one of life's most powerful lessons about ownership. Yusuf grew up facing immense hardships. Poverty surrounded his childhood, opportunities were scarce, and his future seemed limited. If anyone had reasons to feel bitter, stuck, or victimized, it was Yusuf.

Yet, when I met him, he was thriving. Yusuf owned a successful small business, lived comfortably, and radiated an uncommon confidence and peace. Curious, I asked him one day:

"Given all your challenges, how did you build the life you have now?"

Yusuf smiled calmly and replied, "Because I took ownership—not blame."

His answer struck me deeply. Yusuf understood something powerful that many people never learn: the difference between blame and responsibility.

Most people spend their lives assigning blame, explaining their struggles, and justifying their limitations. Yusuf refused to waste energy on blame. Instead, he accepted full ownership of his circumstances—even those he hadn't created. He believed the future was his to shape, no matter how challenging the past.

Why Blame Is So Seductive

Blame feels comforting because it shifts responsibility away from us. If our struggles aren't our fault, we feel safer. We can avoid risk, vulnerability, and action, waiting instead for someone else to change our lives.

Many people, consciously or unconsciously, live this way. They blame their parents, their circumstances, their employers, the economy, or society itself. And often, these complaints are valid. Life isn't always fair, and many people start with genuine disadvantages.

But blame, however justified, never builds a better future. Blame gives you comfort but steals your power. Every moment spent blaming others is a moment not spent building solutions, creating opportunities, or taking action.

Blame keeps you stuck in the past. Ownership propels you toward the future.

Ownership Isn't Fault—It's Freedom

Personal ownership doesn't mean accepting blame for everything. You aren't responsible for every difficulty you've faced. You didn't create many of your challenges, and you shouldn't feel guilty about circumstances outside your control.

Ownership isn't about fault—it's about freedom. It's about deciding to shape your future regardless of who caused the past. You can't control what happened to you, but you can always control how you respond to it.

Yusuf didn't choose his early hardships, but he chose his response. He took ownership of his life, recognizing that no one else could shape his future for him. He didn't waste energy blaming circumstances; instead, he channeled that energy into creating opportunities. Ownership liberated him from the past, enabling him to build the life he wanted.

Victimhood: The Quiet Trap

Many people unknowingly trap themselves in victimhood. They see themselves as helpless victims of circumstance rather than powerful agents of change. Victimhood provides temporary comfort, but it comes at a heavy cost—your power, agency, and potential.

When you identify as a victim, you quietly give away control. You become passive, waiting for external forces—people, opportunities, or circumstances—to change your life. And the longer you wait, the more powerless you feel.

Yusuf understood this subtle yet powerful trap. He refused to see himself as a victim. Instead, he recognized himself as a builder, a creator, someone who could reshape circumstances rather than be shaped by them.

The Power of Radical Responsibility

The moment you embrace full personal ownership, your life transforms dramatically. Responsibility shifts your mindset from passive to proactive, from waiting to creating.

Radical responsibility means acknowledging:

- Your choices shape your life, not your circumstances.
- Your actions create your future, not your past.
- Your decisions today build tomorrow, regardless of yesterday's challenges.

This mindset transforms your identity. Instead of seeing yourself as powerless, you become empowered. Instead of blaming others, you focus on your own actions. Instead of waiting for permission, you give yourself authority.

Responsibility gives you the courage, clarity, and control to build your desired future, regardless of past or present difficulties.

Turning Responsibility into Action

Yusuf didn't just take responsibility—he took action. He started with small, practical steps: learning new skills, seeking mentors, reading books, investing small amounts consistently, and launching small business experiments. Each action built confidence and momentum, transforming responsibility from abstract theory into practical progress.

Taking ownership doesn't require grand gestures or massive changes. It simply requires small, consistent steps forward. Each action reinforces your new identity as someone who builds their future, rather than someone who waits for it.

The New Identity of Ownership

Eventually, ownership becomes more than actions—it becomes your identity. You no longer see yourself as helpless, disadvantaged, or stuck. You see yourself as empowered, capable, and proactive.

This shift in identity changes everything. It influences your daily decisions, your confidence, and your future possibilities. You become someone who builds rather than complains, who acts rather than waits, who creates rather than excuses.

Yusuf's journey didn't just build his wealth—it built his identity. He became someone who creates opportunities rather than waiting for them. He understood deeply that ownership isn't just a choice—it's who you become.

Ownership is Your Greatest Power

Your life today may reflect past circumstances beyond your control. But your life tomorrow is built by your choices today. Ownership means understanding clearly that you—and only you—shape your future.

Don't waste another moment blaming circumstances or waiting for conditions to improve. Take radical responsibility today, start small, and build deliberately. Your future isn't determined by what's behind you—it's shaped by the ownership you embrace right now.

Ownership isn't fault—it's freedom. Your life transforms the moment you understand this truth clearly and act upon it courageously.

Take full ownership. Your future depends on it.

Reflection

Reflection transforms insight into powerful action. Take a moment now and honestly reflect:

1. **What areas of your life have you blamed others or circumstances for instead of taking ownership?**
   Be honest about where blame has kept you stuck or passive.

2. **What emotional comfort has blaming provided?**
   Has blame allowed you to avoid responsibility, risk, or action?

3. **What specific area of your life can you take radical responsibility for today?**
   Identify one clear, practical step toward personal ownership.

Chapter 10

The Comparison Trap

The Cost of the Constant Comparison

When I first launched my side hustle, I found myself scrolling through other entrepreneurs' success stories late at night. Their sleek offices, six-figure launches, and lavish vacations made my small wins feel meaningless. I thought, *If everyone else is doing so well, I must be doing something wrong.*

Comparison felt motivating at first, but quickly morphed into paralyzing envy. I spent more time measuring my progress against others than building my own. Meanwhile, my sales stagnated and my self-esteem cratered.

Social Media's Highlight Reel

Modern life hands us a daily stream of other people's highlights—Instagram filters, LinkedIn milestones, Facebook check-ins. We see the finish line, not the grind leading there.

- **Selective Sharing:** We share promotions, not pay cuts. We post breakthroughs, not breakdowns.
- **False Benchmarks:** We compare our behind-the-scenes with everyone else's final draft.

When your reality never matches the edited versions of others, you start believing you're abnormal—lazy, unlucky, or incompetent.

11.3 Comparison Steals Joy and Focus

Every time you measure your journey by someone else's yardstick, you steal focus from your own path. You trade energy spent on creation for energy spent on critique. You begin chasing other people's dreams instead of tending your own.

Imagine tending your garden while constantly peeking over the fence at your neighbor's roses. You'll never nurture your own blooms.

Reclaiming Your Lane

The antidote to comparison is **focus** and **gratitude**.

- **Focus on Inputs, Not Outcomes:** Celebrate the processes you control—daily habits, small wins, learning curves.

- **Gratitude for Progress:** Keep a weekly log of your achievements, however small, and review it whenever doubt creeps in.

Comparison doesn't vanish overnight. It's a habit you unlearn by consciously returning your attention to your own goals.

Reflection

1. When did you last compare your progress to someone else's—and how did it make you feel?

2. What unique strengths, resources, or wins are you overlooking while fixating on others?

3. What one practice will you commit to this week to refocus on your own journey?

Chapter 11
You Are the Average of Five People

The Company You Keep

My college roommate, Amal, was surrounded by ambitious, supportive friends. Together they studied late, shared job leads, and celebrated each other's successes. No surprise—they all graduated into solid careers and continued to thrive.

Contrast that with my next co-working space, where I met well-meaning peers who enjoyed casual banter, endless coffee breaks, and comfort-zone thinking. Within months, my own drive dulled, and I found myself skipping goals in favor of small talk.

Proximity Shapes Mindsets

Research shows you tend to absorb the habits, beliefs, and even the financial health of those closest to you. If four of your five closest friends live paycheck-to-paycheck, you'll normalize that pattern. If they invest and save, you'll pick up those behaviors too.

Curating Your Inner Circle

You don't need to sever friendships, but you do need **curation**:

- **Add Positive Influences:** Seek out mentors, masterminds, or thoughtfully chosen online communities that model growth.

- **Limit Draining Time:** Gracefully reduce time spent in groups that reinforce scarcity, fear, or inertia.

Gradually, you'll notice your ambitions align with your new averages, and your habits shift accordingly.

Reflection

1. Who are your five closest influences right now?

2. Which of those people uplift your growth—and which hold you back?

3. What steps can you take to add one new high-growth connection this month?

Chapter 12
Procrastination – The Silent Thief of Time

The Cost of "Just One More Day"

Every week, I promised myself, *"Tomorrow I'll start writing the next chapter."* Tomorrow would come—and go. Eventually, I realized I'd lost months to that familiar refrain.

Procrastination isn't laziness; it's fear playing out as delay. Fear of failure, fear of success, fear of stepping into the unknown.

Understanding the Procrastination Loop

- **Avoidance:** You feel discomfort about a task.
- **Distraction:** You soothe that discomfort—social media, snacks, errands.
- **Guilt:** You know you're avoiding, which creates more discomfort.
- **Cycle:** You avoid again to escape guilt.

This loop steals both time and confidence.

Break the Cycle with Micro-Actions

Combat procrastination with **tiny steps**:

- **Two-Minute Rule:** If a task takes two minutes or less, do it immediately.
- **Time Blocks:** Commit to 10 minutes of focused work—then decide if you'll continue.

- ☐ **Public Commitment:** Tell someone you'll complete a task by a specific time to add accountability.

Action dissolves fear and builds momentum.

Reflection

1. **What important task have you been postponing—and why?**
2. **Which discomfort are you avoiding by procrastinating?**
3. **What micro-action will you take in the next two minutes to begin?**

Chapter 13
The Luck Lie

When "Luck" Becomes an Excuse

My friend Omar often lamented, *"I'd be successful if I just got a break."* He watched peers catch viral trends, land fortunate deals, or be in the right place at the right time.

While luck exists, attributing your lack of progress solely to "bad luck" is a **narrative trap**. It absolves you of responsibility and leaves you waiting for external forces.

Creating Your Own Luck

Research on "career serendipity" shows that luck often favors the **prepared mind**:

- **Exposure:** Cultivate diverse networks to increase chance encounters.
- **Skill Development:** The more capable you are, the more opportunities you'll spot and seize.
- **Action Orientation:** Taking even imperfect action opens doors luck never could—because action creates visibility.

From Passive Waiting to Active Creation

Reframe luck from a random gift to a byproduct of effort and presence. Every connection you make, every skill you hone, every goal you pursue is an opportunity magnet.

Reflection

1. Where have you attributed a setback to "bad luck"?

2. What preparations or actions could have increased your "luck advantage"?

3. What one step will you take this week to expand your exposure and readiness?

Chapter 14
You've Been Trained to Stay Broke

A few years ago, I met a young man named Ibrahim who forever changed my understanding of how deeply poverty thinking can be programmed. Ibrahim was smart, motivated, and talented—but financially, he was stuck in a cycle of constant struggle and scarcity. No matter how hard he worked or how carefully he planned, he never seemed to break free from financial hardship.

Frustrated and exhausted, Ibrahim once asked me:

"Why does being broke always feel inevitable?"

As we talked, it became clear: Ibrahim wasn't struggling because he lacked ambition or effort. He was struggling because he had unknowingly been trained to stay broke. From childhood, Ibrahim had absorbed lessons about money, wealth, and possibility that quietly programmed him for financial difficulty.

This poverty programming wasn't obvious or deliberate—but it was powerful, persistent, and deeply destructive. Ibrahim was merely living out patterns he had learned early and unconsciously.

How Poverty Programming Begins

Your beliefs about money, wealth, and success aren't formed randomly—they're learned. From childhood, you absorb subtle but powerful lessons from family, friends, teachers, and society:

"Money doesn't grow on trees."
"We can't afford that."
"Rich people are selfish."

"Be realistic—wealth isn't meant for people like us."

These messages seem innocent, even wise. Yet they quietly shape your beliefs, expectations, and behaviors around money. They train you to see scarcity as normal, struggle as inevitable, and wealth as something reserved for others.

Ibrahim grew up hearing these messages frequently. They became his default beliefs, quietly sabotaging every financial decision he made as an adult. He didn't consciously choose poverty—he had been subtly trained into it.

Scarcity Thinking: The Invisible Cage

The most dangerous aspect of poverty programming is its subtlety. It doesn't announce itself clearly; instead, it quietly shapes your thoughts, decisions, and identity.

Ibrahim saw opportunities through a scarcity lens. Every business idea felt risky. Every investment felt dangerous. He unconsciously viewed money as scarce, limited, and difficult to earn. These beliefs weren't rational—but they were powerful.

Scarcity thinking quietly sabotages potential by convincing you opportunities are rare, resources are limited, and risks are dangerous. This mindset keeps you stuck in cycles of small thinking, fear-driven choices, and constant financial anxiety.

Breaking free begins with understanding clearly that scarcity isn't reality—it's programming.

Trained to Obey, Not Create

Traditional education subtly trains you for obedience rather than creation. You're taught to memorize facts, follow instructions, and seek approval. While these skills have their place, they don't encourage financial independence, risk-taking, or wealth-building.

Ibrahim had absorbed this obedience mindset deeply. He believed wealth required permission, validation, or extraordinary talent. He waited patiently for external approval rather than taking initiative, seeking permission instead of creating opportunities.

But wealth isn't built through obedience—it's built through creativity, initiative, and courage. To escape poverty programming, you must recognize clearly that you don't need permission to build wealth. Your life and wealth-building journey depend entirely on your willingness to act boldly, creatively, and independently.

The Comfort of Familiarity

Poverty programming is difficult to break because it feels comfortable and familiar. Even when uncomfortable or difficult, familiarity provides emotional security. Ibrahim struggled financially—but that struggle was familiar. It matched his childhood experience, his identity, and his expectations.

Stepping outside familiar patterns feels deeply uncomfortable—even frightening. Wealth-building requires embracing uncertainty, risk, and change—feelings that directly conflict with poverty programming. Many people unconsciously sabotage their own success simply to maintain emotional familiarity.

To build wealth, you must become comfortable being uncomfortable. You must deliberately choose growth, risk, and uncertainty over familiarity, comfort, and security. Your financial future depends on your willingness to break free from what's familiar.

Rewriting the Script

The good news is that poverty programming, once recognized clearly, can be rewritten. Your financial future isn't dictated by your past—it's determined by your willingness to challenge old beliefs and deliberately rewrite new ones.

Ibrahim began deliberately challenging his scarcity thinking. He consciously replaced old messages about money with new, empowering beliefs:

- "Money is abundant and accessible."
- "Opportunities are everywhere if I look."

- "I am fully capable of building wealth."

Each new belief transformed his mindset, behaviors, and decisions. He began taking small financial risks, seeking opportunities, and creating instead of waiting. His financial situation improved steadily—not overnight, but significantly and permanently.

You have the same power. The script you've inherited isn't fixed—it's editable. You can rewrite your financial beliefs clearly, deliberately, and powerfully.

You Are the Break in the Pattern

Your family history doesn't determine your financial future—you do. You can choose to break generational patterns of poverty, struggle, and scarcity. Ibrahim's journey wasn't just personal—it was generational. By rewriting his financial story, he rewrote the story for his children, grandchildren, and every future generation.

Breaking poverty programming isn't just about your life—it's about the legacy you leave behind. You have the opportunity and responsibility to become the break in the pattern, the turning point in your family's financial trajectory.

Your journey matters more than you realize. Choose clearly and courageously. The future depends on you.

Reflection

Reflection turns insight into powerful action. Take a moment now and honestly reflect:

1. **What specific poverty messages did you learn growing up?**
   Identify clearly the beliefs you absorbed about money, wealth, and possibilities.

2. **How have these beliefs quietly shaped your financial decisions as an adult?**
   Reflect honestly on patterns of scarcity, fear, or hesitation.

3. **What empowering financial beliefs can you consciously adopt starting today?**

Chapter 15
How to Build Wealth from Zero

The first time I realized I could build wealth without already being wealthy was a revelation. Like many people, I assumed I needed a big inheritance, a high-paying job, or sheer luck. But when I finally looked deeper, I saw countless stories of ordinary individuals who started from nothing—yet climbed to significant financial security.

One person I met, Rashid, embodied this truth perfectly. Rashid began with no savings, no assets, and no college degree. He worked part-time at a grocery store and lived paycheck to paycheck. On paper, nothing set him apart from millions of others who struggle just to cover basic bills.

Yet over a decade later, Rashid owned his home, operated two successful small businesses, and built an investment portfolio. When I asked how he did it, his answer was surprisingly simple: "I stopped believing I needed money to make money. I used what I had—my time, willingness to learn, and determination to keep going."

Rashid's story isn't unique, nor is it magic. It's a reminder that **wealth doesn't start with money—it starts with behavior**. You can build wealth starting from zero if you shift your mindset, adopt the right habits, and take consistent action over time.

The Myth of "I Need Money to Make Money"

One of the most destructive beliefs is that you can't start building wealth without already having it. This myth keeps people stuck, convinced they're doomed to struggle until luck or some financial miracle arrives.

Yet many who have built financial stability started with little or nothing. They didn't wait for a windfall—they created progress by leveraging three powerful assets everyone can access: **time, skills, and focus**.

- **Time**: Even if you have minimal money, you still have hours in your week you can dedicate to learning, creating, or launching something on the side.

- **Skills**: You can develop or monetize a skill—writing, editing, teaching, coding, designing, baking—and offer it online.

- **Focus**: By concentrating on one small, income-producing idea, you can steadily build momentum, credibility, and consistent earnings.

Wealth doesn't start with capital. It starts with using what you already have in new ways.

Mindset Over Money

When you're starting from zero, your biggest obstacle isn't actually money—it's mindset. Rashid recognized early that if he acted like someone who was trapped, he'd stay trapped. Instead, he acted like someone with the potential to learn, grow, and create value.

That meant reading finance books from the library, watching free tutorials online, and practicing new skills daily. Rashid didn't see his lack of money as a dead end—he saw it as an opportunity to learn how to create and multiply value.

Shifting your mindset from "I'm broke" to "I'm building" is the critical first step. This shift pushes you to look for opportunities instead of excuses, to see resources in places you hadn't noticed, and to develop the confidence to try.

Start Small and Simple

Building wealth from zero doesn't require grand gestures. In fact, the smaller and simpler your starting actions, the better. Trying to leap too high too fast often leads to overwhelm or failure.

- **Pick one monetizable skill**: Identify something people will pay for, even if it's just $20 for a small job.

- **Offer that skill online**: Websites like Fiverr, Upwork, or local Facebook groups let you find clients quickly.
- **Reinvest your early earnings**: Instead of spending your first $50, use it to upgrade a tool, learn a new skill, or run a simple ad.
- **Celebrate small wins**: Each small sale or job completed builds your confidence and identity as a wealth-builder.

Slow, consistent progress matters more than dramatic leaps. Every small step removes an excuse and adds to your momentum.

Leverage Compounding Time

When you have minimal funds, you can still invest time in ways that multiply. For instance:

- **Creating Digital Products**: Write an eBook, design templates, record tutorials. Once created, these can sell repeatedly without extra time.
- **Building an Online Presence**: Post valuable content related to your skill or niche. Over time, your audience grows, bringing more clients or sales.
- **Collaborating**: Partner with others who have complementary skills or audiences. Collaboration often opens doors faster than solitary efforts.

Instead of paying money to multiply your resources, you pay with consistent effort over time. And when time compounds—just like money does—you start generating returns that exceed your initial investment of energy.

Save and Invest Even Small Amounts

People often believe saving or investing isn't worth it with tiny amounts. They think $10 saved per week is meaningless. Yet over time, these small, consistent amounts compound into substantial sums.

Rashid started by saving just $20 a month. That's all he could spare. But each month, that $20 went straight into an investment account, earning compound returns. Over several years, that small habit built surprising momentum, fueling bigger gains as he increased his income.

Even $5 saved or invested each week is better than zero. When you're starting from zero, the habit itself is more valuable than the amount. You're training your brain to multiply every small resource you have.

The Power of Focus and Persistence

Starting from zero demands focus—intentionally tuning out distractions and negativity. It's easy to feel discouraged or compare yourself to others. But wealth is rarely built overnight. It's a slow process of repeated, focused effort.

Rashid admitted he nearly quit countless times when progress felt slow. But each day, he reminded himself that every small improvement was compounding. He refused to chase quick fixes or mindless spending. Instead, he channeled his time and energy into building something real, step by step.

Wealth-building from zero can feel daunting, but consistent, focused effort is the ultimate multiplier. Over months and years, those small efforts become something you couldn't have imagined at the start.

You're Not Behind—You're Early

One crucial mindset shift: you're not behind because you have nothing; you're early. You haven't locked yourself into high expenses or complicated liabilities yet. Your advantage is the freedom to experiment, learn, and pivot without huge downside risks.

Rashid didn't see his lack of money as a handicap—he saw it as a chance to build from scratch without inherited debts or entanglements. Embracing your early stage as an advantage frees you from shame, letting you channel energy into creative action.

You can test ideas, fail fast, and adapt quickly because you're not weighed down by large commitments. Often, those with the least end up building the strongest entrepreneurial muscles, precisely because they have to innovate to succeed.

Reflection

It's time to apply what you've learned. Reflect honestly on these questions:

1. **What resources—skills, time, or connections—are you overlooking?**
   Identify hidden assets you can use to start creating value.

2. **What small, consistent habit can you begin today to save or invest?**
   Even if it's just $5 or $10 a week—commit to starting.

3. **Which tiny step can you take to monetize one of your skills or passions?**
   Don't wait for perfection. Launch a small offer, service, or digital product now.

THE 30-DAY WEALTH RESET PLAN

Chapter 16
The 30-Day Wealth Reset Plan

Khadija always felt overwhelmed by her finances. Despite trying various books and programs, she rarely stuck with anything long enough to see real change. Then, one day, she tried a different approach: she gave herself exactly thirty days to do as many small, specific tasks as possible to reset her relationship with money.

The impact was dramatic. In just a month, Khadija radically changed her habits, clarified her goals, and even found a new source of side income. She called it her "30-Day Wealth Reset"—a focused sprint that finally broke her pattern of endless planning and inconsistency.

This chapter is about helping you do the same. You don't need a miracle or a windfall to change your financial life. Sometimes, all you need is a short burst of intentional action—thirty days of unwavering focus—to transform your momentum.

Why 30 Days?

A month is short enough to feel urgent, yet long enough to see tangible progress. Most people can commit to thirty days of consistent action if they know there's an end date. It's a perfect window to test new habits, challenge old beliefs, and create a fresh start.

Khadija recognized this. She knew she could handle almost anything for a month. By clearly defining that window, she removed the pressure of perfection or long-term endurance. Instead, she focused on each day's small tasks, trusting that daily action would compound into meaningful change by day thirty.

Week 1: Reset Your Money Mindset

- **Day 1: Identify Your Money Story**
  Write out the beliefs, fears, and habits you've internalized about money. See them plainly, without judgment.

- **Day 2: Rewrite the Script**
  For each limiting belief, create a positive counter-belief. For instance, *"I'm bad with money"* becomes *"I'm learning how to manage money effectively."*

- **Day 3: Positive Inputs Only**
  Spend today consuming only uplifting or educational content about finances (podcasts, videos, articles). Avoid negative news or gossip.

- **Day 4: Affirmation Anchors**
  Write down a personal money affirmation (e.g., "I build wealth consistently"). Say it out loud each morning and evening.

- **Day 5: Track All Expenses**
  For the next 24 hours, track every purchase—no matter how small. Awareness is your starting point.

- **Day 6: Gratitude Check**
  List five financial blessings you already have—however small. Gratitude calms financial anxiety and resets your mindset for possibility.

- **Day 7: Debrief and Reflect**
  Look back on the week. Which limiting beliefs felt strongest? Which new beliefs started to resonate?

Week 2: Build Habits That Stick

- **Day 8: The $10 Challenge**
  Commit to saving or investing at least $10 today—no excuses. Prove to yourself you can always save something.

- **Day 9: Morning Money Ritual**
  Spend five minutes each morning reviewing your bank balance and any expenses. This small habit builds awareness and control.

- **Day 10: Automate One Action**
  Automate $5, $10, or $20 weekly into a savings or investment account. Remove the daily decision-making.

- **Day 11: Swap a Habit**
  Identify one costly daily habit (like buying coffee) and replace it with a cheaper or free alternative for just today. Notice how it feels.

- **Day 12: Consume Less, Create More**
  Instead of scrolling social media, spend 30 minutes creating something you could sell or share (writing, design, planning a service).

- **Day 13: Weekly Check-In**
  Set aside 15 minutes to review your spending, track upcoming bills, and plan next week's financial tasks.

- **Day 14: Debrief and Reflect**
  Which new habit felt easiest to adopt? Which one was hardest? How can you adjust for greater consistency?

Week 3: Multiply Your Income Streams

- **Day 15: Skill Audit**
  List three skills you could monetize (writing, editing, graphic design, coaching, tutoring). Pick one to focus on this week.

- **Day 16: Make an Offer**
  Post or share an offer using that skill. It could be on social media, a freelance platform, or community board. Keep it simple and real.

- **Day 17: Ask for Feedback**
  Reach out to one person to try your service or product—at a discounted rate or even free—just to collect testimonials and refine your approach.

- **Day 18: Create a Simple Payment Method**
  Set up a PayPal, Venmo, or other payment link. Make it easy for people to pay you without hassle.

- **Day 19: Document the Journey**
  Share updates online. Show your process. Ask for support or collaboration. Visibility often brings unexpected opportunities.

- **Day 20: Reinvest Early Earnings**
  If you earn anything, even $20, use part of it to upgrade a tool, fund a small ad, or learn a new skill.

- **Day 21: Debrief and Reflect**
  How did it feel to create or offer something? What worked, and what needs adjusting?

Week 4: Secure and Scale

- **Day 22: Emergency Cushion**
  If you haven't started already, begin an emergency fund, even if it's $50. Knowing you have a small buffer reduces stress.

- **Day 23: Weekly Wealth Hour**
  Block out one hour a week for all things money—reviewing bills, updating budgets, planning financial moves. Make it routine.

- **Day 24: Explore One Investment**
  Spend time learning about a beginner-friendly investment (like an index fund). Commit a small amount—even $5—to start.

- **Day 25: Declutter Financial Distractions**
  Cancel any unused subscriptions. Unfollow accounts that trigger spending. Clean up your digital environment.

- **Day 26: Celebrate Progress**
  Look at how far you've come in three weeks. Acknowledge every small win, every new habit, every mindset shift.

- **Day 27: Vision Board or Journal**
  Capture your future financial goals—owning a home, hitting a savings milestone, or launching a passion project.

- **Day 28: Debrief and Reflect**
  Which changes feel most sustainable? How can you extend these new habits beyond the 30-day window?

Days 29–30: Lock In the Change

- **Day 29: Commit to the Next 90 Days**
  Choose which habits and strategies you'll continue, and set a 90-day goal. The 30-day sprint gave you momentum—now extend it.

- **Day 30: Review, Reward, and Renew**
  Look back at your biggest wins and lessons learned. Reward yourself meaningfully. Then renew your commitment to ongoing growth.

Reflection

Thirty days can change everything if you're consistent. Reflect on your plan:

1. **What blocks have historically stopped you from maintaining financial habits beyond a week or two?**
   Identify how this 30-day structure can help you overcome those blocks.

2. **Which week's focus do you think will challenge you most?**
   Awareness helps you prepare and strategize.

3. **What's one thing you're most excited to learn or accomplish in this 30-day sprint?**

Chapter 17
Stop Spending Like You're Rich

One evening, I spoke with Nadine, a bright professional who seemed to have her life together. Good job, decent salary, a social circle that admired her. But Nadine carried a secret: she was drowning in debt. Despite earning more than her parents ever had, she had nothing left at the end of each month—just rising bills, unmanageable payments, and mounting stress.

Her confusion was palpable. *"I've done well in my career,"* she admitted, *"but my money just vanishes. I look successful on the outside, but I'm terrified inside."*

Digging deeper, Nadine realized she was **spending money to look rich**—not to **be** rich. She wasn't trying to brag; she was just numbing stress, chasing validation, and maintaining appearances that felt expected in her social circle. But chasing that image was quietly sabotaging her real financial progress.

Nadine's story isn't unusual. In a culture obsessed with projecting success, countless people silently juggle debt, fear, and shallow spending habits to "keep up." This chapter is about recognizing and breaking that cycle—learning to stop performing wealth and start building it.

Why Looking Rich Is So Tempting

Social media highlights lifestyles that appear elegant, fun, and effortless. Ads promise you'll feel powerful if you drive a luxury car, wear brand-name clothes, or accessorize with the latest tech. Friends share photos of lavish meals, trendy vacations, and fancy gadgets, implicitly suggesting this is normal, even necessary, for social belonging.

It's easy to internalize these messages. A pricey dinner or designer purchase offers a fleeting rush of pleasure, a sense of belonging, or an illusion of success. But beneath the surface, these indulgences often mask deeper insecurities, fears, or the relentless pursuit of external validation.

Performing wealth might temporarily soothe your ego, but it cannot create true financial security—and it regularly prevents it. The more you spend to look rich, the harder it becomes to actually build lasting wealth.

The Lifestyle Creep Trap

For many people, an early sign of "performing wealth" is **lifestyle creep**. This happens when your expenses rise in lockstep with your income. Instead of saving or investing any pay increase, you immediately upgrade your car, apartment, wardrobe, or leisure activities, leaving you with the same financial stress but fancier stuff.

Nadine succumbed to lifestyle creep every time she got a raise. She felt she *deserved* the better apartment, the newest phone, and more frequent weekend getaways. But these automatic upgrades devoured her extra income, locking her into a cycle of perpetual anxiety—even with a respectable salary.

Lifestyle creep feels harmless at first. But over years, it leads to heavy debt, minimal savings, and zero real progress toward financial freedom. Every new expense normalizes quickly, making it tough to revert when reality hits.

The Emotional Cost of Showing Off

Beyond financial damage, performing wealth exacts a high emotional toll:

- **Shame and Secrecy**: You know your lifestyle isn't sustainable, but revealing the truth feels humiliating.

- **Chronic Stress**: Fear of being "found out" or losing the ability to maintain appearances.

- **Identity Conflict**: Struggling between the person you are and the persona you present.

Eventually, the emotional burden grows heavier than the social benefits. Pretending success can leave you feeling like a fraud, constantly anxious about potential collapse.

Choosing to Be Rich Instead of Looking Rich

The turning point for Nadine came when she realized she was exhausted from the performance. She decided she'd rather **be** financially secure than just appear to be. That required a fundamental shift in how she spent, saved, and perceived money.

She scaled back on trendy social events. She downgraded her apartment to free up cash. She stopped using shopping as a stress reliever. Instead, Nadine channeled money into paying down debt, creating a small investment account, and building a modest emergency fund. The "ego hit" was real—her peers noticed she was going out less or sporting fewer luxuries. But Nadine found a surprising relief in letting go of the facade.

Gradually, her real financial picture improved, reducing anxiety and fostering true confidence. Instead of performing wealth, she was building it.

How to Stop Looking Rich and Start Building Wealth

1. **Conduct an Honest Audit**
   List all your expenses for the past three months. Ask yourself: *Did I need this? Or was I performing?* Identify where you spend for image or emotion rather than genuine utility.

2. **Set Realistic Status-Free Goals**
   Define what true wealth means to you: security, freedom, choices, peace of mind. Align your spending with these deeper values, not with fleeting impressions.

3. **Downshift One Lifestyle Choice**
   Pick an expense you suspect is mostly for appearances—like an overly expensive car lease—and downgrade. Reclaim that money for debt reduction or investments.

4. **Automate Real Wealth Behaviors**
   Steadily invest or save each paycheck. Automate these processes so you don't rely on willpower or wait until it's "convenient." Let your money quietly work for you.

5. **Address Emotional Triggers**
   If stress triggers spending, learn alternative coping mechanisms. Try journaling, exercising, or diving into a hobby that doesn't revolve around spending. Looking at underlying emotions helps you break the cycle of performing wealth.

6. **Surround Yourself with Builders, Not Show-Offs**
   If your circle normalizes big spending just for appearance, it's harder to maintain discipline. Seek communities or mentors who value genuine growth, not superficial flexing.

By systematically removing the pressures that compel you to show off, you begin investing in real progress, not empty image.

When Downshifting Feels Like Losing

Downgrading lifestyle expenses can feel like defeat, especially if your self-image is tied to certain luxuries. Nadine admitted feeling embarrassed when she returned her leased luxury car for a simpler used model. But she reframed it: *"I'm not giving up status—I'm buying back my peace."*

Choosing a smaller apartment or cutting high-end brand spending doesn't mean sacrificing your personality or enjoyment. It means cutting superficial costs so you can afford deeper security and future freedom. Your real identity and worth aren't tied to what label you wear, what car you drive, or how much you spend on brunch.

True confidence grows from authenticity and stable finances, not from external validation. Embracing that mindset helps you endure the short-term ego bumps of living below your means.

Reflection

To transform insights into real behavior change, reflect honestly right now:

1. **Where in your life are you mostly performing wealth?**
   Identify expenses made more for image than necessity or genuine enjoyment.

2. **How do these "performance" expenses align with—or detract from—your deeper financial goals?**
   Be candid about the emotional appeal and the hidden cost.

3. **What's one significant spending category you could downgrade immediately for genuine savings or investment?**
   Commit to a first step.

HOW TO STAY RICH
ONCE YOU GET THERE

Chapter 18
How to Stay Rich Once You Get There

Lana used to daydream about the day she'd finally "make it." A natural entrepreneur, she launched a small online clothing store from her living room, hustling for years with minimal returns. Then, almost overnight, it all clicked: her social media went viral, orders exploded, and her income soared beyond anything she'd seen before.

But her success presented a new challenge. Within a year, Lana found herself surprisingly broke again, despite the huge spike in sales. She confessed, *"I always thought getting rich was the hard part—but no one taught me how to handle it once I arrived."*

Lana's story isn't unique. Athletes, lottery winners, business owners—plenty of people achieve financial success for a moment, only to lose it just as quickly. The problem isn't creating wealth; it's **keeping** it.

This chapter is about avoiding the post-success trap: learning to stabilize, protect, and keep growing your money once you "make it."

Why Getting Rich and Staying Rich Are Different Skills

It's tempting to believe that once you've built significant income or wealth, you're set. But money doesn't manage itself. The habits and strategies that helped you rise must evolve to keep you there.

- **Getting Rich** often involves risk-taking, bold moves, hustle, and continuous growth.
- **Staying Rich** requires discipline, systems, protection, and

long-term thinking.

Lana's fall from grace wasn't due to laziness. She continued working hard. But she never developed the specific habits, systems, and mindsets that protect wealth. Instead, she kept scaling her expenses, ignoring bigger-picture strategies, and trusting luck to keep the money flowing.

Wealth, once acquired, must be managed or it will slip away.

Common Pitfalls After Success

1. **Lifestyle Overdrive**
   Once money rolls in, you may feel you've earned the right to splurge without restraint. Costly homes, cars, or luxury habits quickly devour your newfound wealth, leaving you at risk if income dips.

2. **No Systems or Budget**
   It's easy to assume a big bank balance solves your problems, so you skip proper budgeting or tracking. Without systems, overspending or random investing decisions undermine stability.

3. **Ego Takes Over**
   People start treating you differently, and it's easy to believe your own hype. Overconfidence can lead to reckless decisions, poor deals, or ignoring sound advice because you think you're infallible.

4. **Isolation**
   It's common to become more secretive or insular, avoiding honest conversations with financial mentors or peers. Without accountability, it's easy to slide into bad choices unchecked.

Even when you're financially set, these pitfalls can quickly drain your resources, leaving you back where you started—often with more debt and embarrassment than before.

The Power of Systems

One key difference between those who keep wealth and those who lose it is the use of **systems**—automated checks, balances, and habits that ensure money is allocated wisely.

- **Automated Saving and Investing**: Even if you earn large amounts, automation ensures consistent growth.

- **Clear Budgets and Expense Tracking**: Yes, you should still budget, even if you earn plenty. Surprising though it seems, the wealthiest people often keep close tabs on their spending.

- **Risk Management**: Insurance, diversification, legal structures—these guard against unforeseen blows that could derail your progress.

Systems do the heavy lifting, preventing reckless spending or overlooked bills, and creating a safety net for when life inevitably shifts. By installing simple processes—like automatic transfers to investment accounts—your wealth grows without needing constant willpower or decisions.

Staying Humble, Staying Hungry

Another common post-success trap is letting your **ego** overshadow reality. When large sums appear, you might feel invincible, forgetting the humility and discipline that got you there in the first place.

Lana admitted she fell into this. She started dismissing advice, chasing quick opportunities, and ignoring financial red flags because she believed her success was guaranteed. In reality, her new wealth needed careful stewardship, not cavalier decision-making.

Staying rich means maintaining the hunger for learning and improvement. Keep reading, keep talking with mentors, and keep reminding yourself that money, while abundant, isn't infinite if mismanaged.

Diversify Your Assets and Your Identity

When new wealth arrives, it's tempting to keep all your eggs in the same successful basket. But that success might be temporary or vulnerable to market changes, competition, or personal factors.

Smart wealth preservation often involves **diversification**—spreading risk across various asset classes, like real estate, stocks, and business ventures. Even if one area falters, others can stabilize you.

Additionally, diversify your **identity**. Don't tie your entire sense of self to your current business or income stream. Lana realized she was "just the clothing brand person," and when her market dipped, she felt personally crushed. By exploring other interests or developing new projects, you protect not only your finances but also your emotional well-being.

Maintain Accountability and Advice

When you begin earning big, it's normal to worry about who to trust. Yet, going solo is dangerous. Without accountability, it's easy to make hasty choices or get sucked into bad deals.

Instead, seek out:

- **Financial Mentors**: Advisors or successful peers who challenge and guide you.

- **Partners or Groups**: Business or investing groups that foster transparent conversations and shared learning.

- **Close Confidants**: A spouse, partner, or friend you trust to give honest feedback on big decisions.

Having people who aren't star-struck by your wealth helps keep you grounded, inquisitive, and honest with yourself.

The New Normal: Confidence with Caution

Staying rich doesn't mean living in fear. It means living with **confidence tempered by caution**. Confidence in your ability to create and manage money. Caution in acknowledging that markets shift, unexpected events happen, and no stream of income is invincible.

Lana, after regaining her balance, described it this way: *"I had to become both bold and careful at once—bold enough to keep moving forward, careful enough not to let success blind me."* She built systems that automatically saved and invested parts of her income, set limits on lifestyle spending, and assembled a small circle of trusted advisors who helped her navigate growth responsibly.

Reflection

Pause here to integrate these insights. Whether you're nearing significant wealth or preparing for it, think about how you'll protect and sustain your growth.

1. **Which pitfalls—lifestyle overdrive, no systems, ego, or isolation—feel most likely for you?**
   Understanding your vulnerability is the first step to prevention.

2. **What systems—automated saving, budgeting, or legal structures—do you need to implement or improve?**
   Commit to at least one immediate system upgrade.

3. **How will you remain accountable and humble?**
   Who can you trust for honest feedback, and how often will you check in?

HOW TO TEACH WEALTH TO YOUR CHILDREN

Chapter 19
How to Teach Wealth to Your Children (or Future Self)

A few years ago, I attended a small community gathering on financial literacy, where I met Saeed—a quiet, thoughtful man who seemed particularly invested in one theme of the discussion: *teaching wealth principles to the next generation.* After the event, Saeed told me a story about how he wished his parents had prepared him better for the realities of money, work, and independence.

He recalled how, as a child, he only heard phrases like "We can't afford that" and "Money is hard to come by," but no one ever taught him how to save, invest, or think proactively about income. No one explained the difference between assets and liabilities or how to leverage time and compound interest. As he entered adulthood, Saeed realized he was stumbling in the dark, repeating the same scarce patterns he had unconsciously absorbed.

It wasn't until he began teaching himself financial basics in his late twenties—through books, free online courses, and trial and error—that Saeed broke the cycle. He vowed to share what he learned with others, especially the children in his extended family, so they wouldn't have to start from scratch. His resolve planted a question in my mind: How many of us wish our parents had taught us the mechanics—and the mindset—of building wealth when we were young?

The truth is, every child deserves more than silence and vague fears about money. They deserve honest conversations, practical tools, and an understanding of wealth that can shape their future positively. And if you don't have children, imagine passing these lessons to *your future self,* ensuring the adult you become (or want to become) has a clearer financial path than your younger version ever did.

Why Teaching Wealth Matters

Whether you have children or not, consider the power of legacy: what you pass on to those who follow you, or to your *future self* as you evolve. Teaching wealth principles isn't just about money; it's about confidence, resilience, and the ability to dream bigger. When children—or your younger self—understand money early, they can:

- Avoid the pitfalls of debt and unrestrained spending.

- Develop a sense of agency—knowing they can create income, not just consume.

- Resist the scarcity mindset that plagues so many adults.

Imagine how different your path might have been if you'd learned these truths at age 10 or 15. That's the gift you can give to children now—or to the version of you still growing, still forming new habits and beliefs.

Start with Their (or Your) Current Reality

Children learn by seeing, not just hearing. So do adults, for that matter. If you're teaching wealth principles to a child, don't just lecture about saving or investing—show them your own budget, your own approach to saving, even if it's modest. If you're teaching your *future self,* start by applying these lessons in small, visible ways—like tracking daily expenses or setting up a beginner-friendly investment account.

- **Show, don't just tell**: If you tell a child saving is important but never demonstrate how you save, they'll likely repeat what you *do,* not what you say.

- **Model the journey**: If you want your future self to manage money differently, start with clear daily actions—journaling your spending, reading a finance book, or automating small investments.

Narratives are powerful. Share stories about how you (or someone else) struggled financially and overcame obstacles by learning specific wealth principles. Real-life examples resonate more than abstract advice.

Explain Basic Concepts Early

Many children (and unprepared adults) grow up thinking money is either endless or perpetually scarce—often both at once. Bridging that gap starts with simple, foundational lessons:

1. **Money as a Tool**
   Teach that money isn't mysterious or evil; it's a resource for creating and solving problems. It's neutral—how you use it matters.

2. **Spending vs. Saving vs. Investing**
   Even a child can grasp this if framed simply: Some money we use now, some we store for later, and some we put into ideas that make more money over time.

3. **The Power of Compound Interest**
   Explain how savings can grow by earning interest or investments can multiply. Illustrations—like doubling a penny every day—captivate young minds and remind adults of the exponential potential of steady investing.

4. **Earning Through Value**
   Children often believe money appears from ATMs or parents' wallets. Show them how creating value—through work, services, or solving problems—earns income.

If you're teaching your future self, treat these basics as your daily practice. Even if you've read about compound interest or budgeting before, revisit them actively. Reinforce your internal "child"—the part of you still forming habits and beliefs about money.

Make It Practical and Engaging

Theory bores people—young or grown. Learning sticks when it's hands-on and relevant. If you're teaching wealth principles, consider:

- **Mini Entrepreneurial Experiments**
  Encourage children to sell homemade crafts or run a lemonade stand. For adults, try launching a small online service or product. Even a $5 sale teaches how effort converts to income.

- **Visual Savings Goals**
  Use a clear jar or digital tracker to watch savings grow. When you physically see progress, the lesson becomes tangible. For adults, set up an account that tracks savings or investment milestones visually.

- **Budgeting Made Simple**
  Show them (or your future self) how to create a small budget for a project or outing. Understanding basic budget principles—like planning, allocating, and adjusting—demystifies money management.

- **Reward Consistency, Not Just Big Achievements**
  Both children and our own younger selves thrive on encouragement. Celebrate consistent saving or the first small investment. Confidence cements new habits faster than criticism ever could.

Talk About Wealth Mindset

Most people grow up hearing more about scarcity and bills than about growth and opportunities. Changing the money conversation starts with discussing mindset.

Encourage children—and remember for your future self—**wealth isn't about having fancy things; it's about having choices.** People who build wealth aren't always the smartest or the luckiest; they're often just the ones who refuse to be bound by old limiting beliefs. Stress these points:

- **Failure is Data**: If a money experiment fails, it's not a sign to quit; it's information to learn from.

- **Money Grows with Value**: Earning more often comes from solving bigger problems or helping more people, not just working harder.

- **Adaptability Over Perfection**: The financial world changes; what matters is the willingness to adapt and keep learning.

When children (or your future self) sees money as an active, evolving tool rather than a static source of stress, they embrace challenges instead of fearing them.

Lead with Transparency, Not Perfection

No one's perfect with money. Pretending otherwise undermines trust. If you're teaching children, share real, age-appropriate stories of your financial mistakes and what you learned. If you're teaching your future self, document your missteps so you can reflect and improve. Mistakes become lessons rather than shameful secrets.

Transparency builds credibility. Children respect honesty over hollow lectures, and your own subconscious "learner" self benefits more from candid reflection than forced optimism. Show how you overcame obstacles, adjusted budgets, or learned from investing errors. Realness resonates.

You're Building a Legacy

Whether passing these lessons to children or to your evolving self, remember: it's not about perfection. It's about planting seeds of understanding, confidence, and possibility that can grow over time.

Saeed, the quiet man from the community gathering, now mentors his nephews and nieces. He shows them how to budget birthday money, explains compound interest with a mason jar of pennies, and encourages them to start tiny businesses selling homemade crafts. They're not just learning numbers; they're absorbing a mindset of empowerment, creativity, and self-reliance.

Imagine if you did the same for yourself five years ago—or if you do it now for the version of you five years from today. You'd accelerate your growth and rewrite your money story more intentionally. That's the power of passing on wealth principles—*to the next generation or to your own future self.*

Reflection

Take a moment to reflect on how you can teach or reinforce these lessons:

1. **Who needs these wealth principles—your children, siblings, or even your future self?**
   Be clear about who you're guiding.

2. **Which core financial concepts would you prioritize sharing?**
   Saving, investing, budgeting, entrepreneurial thinking, or mindset?

3. **What practical, age-appropriate or skill-appropriate steps can you introduce first?**
   Think about small wins that build curiosity and confidence.

Conclusion
Your New Financial Story

When I first started writing this book, I hoped to shed light on a painful truth many people experience but rarely confront: *being poor isn't just about money—it's about the unexamined beliefs, habits, and environments that quietly keep you stuck.* Over the course of these chapters, we've ventured through the subtle traps of poverty programming, comfort zones, endless excuses, toxic surroundings, and unseen habits. We've explored the difference between trading time for money and building true ownership, and we've revealed how fear, blame, and unexamined desires sabotage real progress.

Yet throughout every section, a core message has emerged: **You are not doomed by your circumstances. You have the power to rewrite your money story.**

It's easy to feel overwhelmed in a world where financial stress seems more common than financial peace, where everyone appears to be hustling but few truly succeed, and where messages of lack and limitation can drown out your ambition. But true freedom starts when you decide to question the script you inherited and reclaim your capacity to build, save, invest, and grow.

A Journey of Layers

Think back to Chapter 1, where we explored how you were probably programmed long before you had a say in the matter. You didn't choose your earliest money beliefs, yet they governed your decisions for years—maybe decades. Recognizing that script was your first act of rebellion.

From there, each chapter peeled away a layer:

- **Comfort,** that silent killer of growth, which keeps you numb rather than content.

- **Excuses,** those intelligent-sounding lies that shield you from risk but also from progress.

- **Environment,** the subtle background that either nurtures or poisons your financial potential.

- **Habits,** those daily repeats that compound into an inevitable result—good or bad.

- **Misunderstood Money,** which we so often treat emotionally instead of strategically.

- **Hard Work Without Leverage,** which can leave you exhausted and underpaid indefinitely.

- **Fear of Starting,** paralyzing you before you even begin.

- **Ownership,** where you reclaim control by refusing to blame circumstances, empowering yourself to create real change.

- **Poverty Training,** the generational curse that can be broken with your intentional action.

And then the **Bonus Chapters** offered deeper dives: building wealth from zero, resetting your finances in 30 days, teaching essential wealth lessons to your children (or your evolving self), stopping the cycle of performing wealth, and finally learning how to stay rich once you achieve it.

It All Comes Down to Ownership and Action

Across every story and example, two themes stand out:

1. **Own Your Choices**: Nothing changes if you don't own your current reality. Blame or victimhood can temporarily soothe your ego, but they steal your power to act. Ownership is about accepting where you are—even if it's unfair or difficult—so you can shape what happens next.

2. **Act, Even Imperfectly**: Understanding your situation is essen-

tial, but it remains inert without action. Small, flawed steps are better than permanent inertia. Fear loses its grip, excuses lose their voice, and habits can be broken or rebuilt only through consistent doing.

Every chapter's reflection and journal prompts have aimed to spark these two key behaviors: **take responsibility** and **take a step**—no matter how small.

Your Future Is Unwritten

Despite past programming, self-sabotage, or missed opportunities, your future remains open. You have every reason to believe that your dreams—homeownership, debt freedom, a thriving business, or simply sleeping without financial anxiety—can be realized if you consistently apply the lessons you've embraced here.

No book alone can guarantee your success. Transformation ultimately arises from daily, conscious decisions: how you spend your mornings, what financial habits you maintain, how you interpret challenges, and who you let shape your mindset.

As you move forward, you'll still face hurdles. Life will throw surprises, and old habits will tempt you to revert. But now you carry a blueprint—a deeper awareness of why you've struggled and how to rewire those struggles into strengths.

Start (Again) Right Now

If there's one final suggestion to reinforce, it's this: **commit to a small action today.** Not tomorrow, not "someday," but right this moment. Open a savings account, list a small product or service for sale, review your expenses for the week, share your financial goals with a trusted friend—anything that shifts knowledge into momentum.

Tomorrow, do it again. And the next day, another step. Before long, the very scripts that once defined you will become distant memories, replaced by new habits, beliefs, and environments that support genuine financial freedom.

A Final Word of Encouragement

You've come a long way already—simply by reading, reflecting, and daring to challenge old patterns. That in itself is a victory. Recognize your growth and celebrate each insight. You're no longer sleepwalking through inherited limitations; you're awake, aware, and armed with practical strategies.

Remember Nadine, Jamal, Amina, Rashid, and the many real-life examples woven throughout these chapters. None of them achieved a frictionless fairytale. They confronted the same fears, habits, and doubts you might have. But they persisted with ownership and consistent, if imperfect, action. Over time, they reshaped their financial destinies, proving that transformation is possible for anyone who refuses to surrender.

The same can be true for you—no matter your starting point, no matter how hopeless it has felt. Your story isn't locked. It's alive, changing with every decision you make.

Now the Story Is Yours

You hold the pen of your financial future. Will you continue an old narrative of limitations, or will you write a new script where excuses fade, comfort zones expand, and disciplined ownership leads to real wealth?

The chapters may end here, but your financial journey continues. Take the lessons, keep them alive in your daily habits and decisions, share them with those around you, and allow each small act of courage to accumulate into the wealth, security, and freedom you deserve.

Your future is waiting—*go build it.*

Thank you for reading, reflecting, and daring to rewrite your money story. May you carry these insights forward, not just for your own prosperity, but for everyone inspired by your journey. The best is yet to come.

www.ingramcontent.com/pod-product-compliance
Lightning Source LLC
Chambersburg PA
CBHW071217070526
44584CB00019B/3062